The Thoughts

The Thoughts

Sarah Barnsley

smith|doorstop

the poetry business

Published 2022 by The Poetry Business
Campo House,
54 Campo Lane,
Sheffield S1 2EG
www.poetrybusiness.co.uk

ISBN 978-1-914914-02-7
eBook ISBN 978-1-914914-03-4

Designed & typeset by The Poetry Business.
Printed by Imprint Digital.

British Library Cataloguing-in-Publication Data.
A catalogue record for this book is available from the British Library.

Smith|Doorstop is a member of Inpress
www.inpressbooks.co.uk.
Distributed by IPS UK, 1 Deltic Avenue,
Rooksley, Milton Keynes MK13 8LD.

The Poetry Business gratefully acknowledges the support
of Arts Council England.

After great pain, a formal feeling comes
– Emily Dickinson, poem 341

We stand upon the brink of a precipice. We peer into the abyss – we grow sick and dizzy. Our first impulse is to shrink from the danger. Unaccountably we remain [...] there grows into palpability, a shape, far more terrible than any genius, or any demon of a tale, and yet it is but a thought, although a fearful one, and one which chills the very marrow of our bones with the fierceness of the delight of its horror. It is merely the idea of what would be our sensations during the sweeping precipitancy of a fall from such a height [...] And because our reason violently deters us from the brink, therefore do we the more impetuously approach it.
– Edgar Allan Poe, 'The Imp of the Perverse'

Contents

Ruminations

Compulsions

Avoidances

Magical Thinking

Thought-Action-Fusion

Formulation

Treatment

Epilogue

For Louise, whose name means Hero

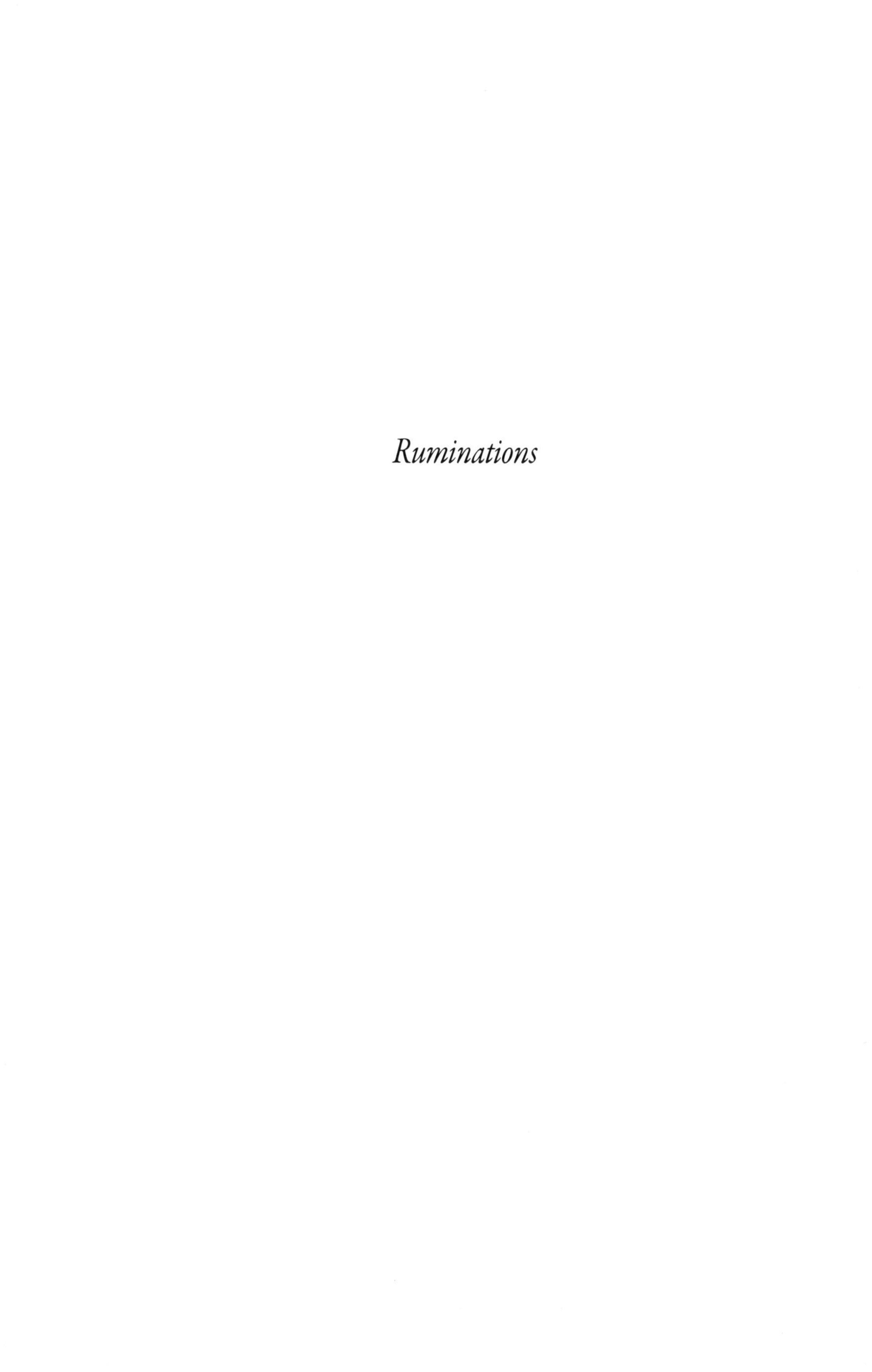

Ruminations

Body Found in Garden After Confession

How the body got there,
or whose it was, nobody knew,

not even the confessor,
who had been resident all their life in Brazil,

who was on holiday in the Bahamas at the time,
experts suggest, that the body entered the earth,

who was on life support after a diving accident
at the point, experts say, that the body's owner died

and *we are pleased to bring this case to its conclusion*
said the Chief Superintendent

and *the nation can feel safe again*
said the Prime Minister

and *we pray for all the families*
said the Archbishop of Canterbury

and the confessor said goodbye to the house, the dog,
took off their shoes, clothes and wedding band,

went out into the garden and
lay as still as a forgotten rake in tall grass.

This Horse

There's this horse
that can't eat apples.
It's not that the horse
doesn't like apples
or that its castle of teeth
can't crush them
or that its leather-satchel tongue
can't collect the bits
or that its upturned welly of a throat
can't tramp down the chunks –

it's that one day,
as it drew up an apple
of no distinction,
the horse had a thought:
What if I choke on this?
And the more the horse tried
to swat the thought away,
the more the apple grew,
and the more the thought grew

until the horse felt it had Jupiter
and all its moons in its mouth
and it couldn't breathe
and it was gagging
and its owner tried to reason with it,
but the horse wouldn't be told
and over the course of a year
the horse visited the vet
every Wednesday at 12

and the vet advised the horse
to try an exercise where the horse
had to choose a small globe
from a bagged assortment

and hold each one in its mouth
in a series of graded steps:
a robin's egg for one minute,
a beetroot for two,
a cannonball for three;

and the horse had to
commit to the process
and *tolerate the discomfort*
and by all means note down
its thoughts and feelings
but not respond to them
and none of this worked
and the only thing for the horse
to do was to eat oats and practise
radical acceptance
of apples as something eaten
by other horses
in another place and time
as if all the apples in the world
were locked behind
glass cabinets
in a museum
with all the other things
the horse's thoughts had
forced it to give up:
cool pools,
hugs of mud,
low-hedged fields.

Tainted Ode

O Dirt, what is this madness, how do you get me going so?
I know you've kissed the necks of bins, a kerb's lips, the skins of
bus seats; my darling dirty Dirt, I know you've kissed a pug's arse.
I think about you all the time, my love. I wait for you every night,
put on clean sheets, wipe down the soles of my slippers, wash my
hands before brushing my teeth, all because of you. I wonder:
what is Dirt doing right now? At parties I glimpse you in the floor
of my glass, in a beard, in a broken arrow of saliva but I know in
my head it's not really you, that you have better things to do, like
sleep your way round town. I love you so much I can't eat
anything that comes out of the ground, throw away tasty in-date
food at the thought of you. People say one day I'll meet the Dirt
of my dreams and then I'll have something real to worry about.
O Dirt, no one can know about us. Meet me one lunchtime,
but no texting; I want no trace of you. Dirt, what does it take
to make you come? What does your face look like when you do?
Dirt, I hate it when you don't get back to me, don't tell me where
you are. Dirt, I'm yours; come, sweep me off my filthy slippers.

The Fugitive

Now I don't know whether to report this
to the British Meteorological Society,
NASA or the police, but I'm telling you

a prison fell into my head, last year, in
broad daylight, in its entirety – walls,
exercise yard, even the bus stop outside.

At first I kept it to myself. I knew it wasn't
right to have something so massive stuck
in my head, but there it was – brown, bricky,

with pinstripe windows draping my retina
and a *Visitor's Entrance* → corkscrewing
my ear canal. And as the cars continued to

drive past, and officers came and went through
the small door cut into the gate like a wooden
shirt pocket, I carried on as usual, got up, went

to work, talked to people in shops, and no one
seemed to see it even though barbed wire was
trellising out of my nostrils; and at particular

times of day, the prison lights would go out
behind my eyes and I'd be in darkness, listening
to the disinterested hum of the outside world.

And the more no one noticed, and the more I
carried on, the taller, the wider, the deeper
the prison became. I learned the name of every

prisoner, acquired the files on all their crimes,
discovered the heartbreak and the pain of them,
their visitors, their victims, the passing thoughts

of support staff, the governor, probation officers,
the whole human pool of everything that had ever
been thought and felt within those walls,

the exercise yard, the bus stop outside, until I came to
myself and heard from someone who had noticed it
and had noticed that it had all, really, been in my head

and nowhere else and said that nothing bad will happen
if I leave it there and can I see that slant of daylight,
the deserted road which leads out of town?

Does This Mean I'm a Steps Fan?

5 in the morning.
I wake up and start masturbating
when Steps come into my head.
Does this mean I'm a Steps fan?

I'm giving a lecture
on an experimental American poet
and I'm about to say something really cool about prosody
when I look at the front row and notice that, alternately, the audience looks
like Faye, Claire, Lee, Lisa and H, on repeat, through
the next row and the next like checked cloth.
Does this mean I'm a Steps fan?

I'm at a funeral
and it's all v. sad and I'm going to do one
of the readings when 'Tragedy', the Steps cover, explodes
in my mind on full blast; and rather than read a nineteenth-century poem
in *the poetry voice*, I feel the urge to wallop out a *TRAGEDY!*
at the distraught mourners complete with dance moves.
Does this mean I'm a Steps or a Bee Gees fan?

I'm compelled to go over
the Steps discography, recall it exactly –
singles, chart position, release date – same for albums, further
differentiating between studio albums and compilations while we have a
slap-up birthday lunch and it doesn't feel good (the slap-up lunch)
and I can't remember it all (the discography).
Am I or am I not a Steps fan?

I crack and see the GP;
Steps have been in my head morning, noon and night.
I note the doctor's tasselled shoes and think there's no way
she's heard of Steps. I tell her my family has this thing and I'm the same,
I've never said anything as I didn't want *questionable music taste*
on my medical records but I need help, I need a diagnosis:
am I a Steps fan?

The day my brain broke

was sunny was warm in the South of France
warm with wine tour was *we're on honeymoon!*
was sunny was changeable warm in the ears
far from home sunny between lightning
was warm was hot brought to boil in a bistro
sunny for everyone else on that tourist train
was suddenly hot torture chamber on wine tour
in hot water suddenly the main character
boiling in jail was changed into a murderer
lightning strike chamber bolt locked in a film
was sunny was warm in the South of France
telling my lover things had gone weird
was hot honeymoon stuck on *le petit train*
warm sunny wine on the old town loop
was stuck in a loop stuck South of France
was sudden was warm was sunny was hot

Compulsions

I come through the door like pest control

scan the usual places, cross-reference
with my hidden clipboard which itemises
the molecular history of the doormat,
the shoes, key hooks and coat rack.

I walk down the hall with my captive
customer and while you talk about how
good it is to be home, my head's in the
white van outside, selecting treatments;

and while my hands put on the kettle,
I'm zipping up a boiler suit on the steps,
twanging the elastic of goggles, latex
gloves, covering everything up.

If only you knew how much pressure
they put me under to complete each job
you wouldn't be asking me to repeat
what you just said, telling me that you

might as well be a cardboard cut-out,
that I act as if *you* are the problem and
I can't listen anyway for I am staring
poison on to the hall floor, thinking

traps into corners, sucking the carpet
into industrial washers just by breathing,
saving us all before bedtime, not even
thinking of taking a penny for my work.

Private and Confidential

Unless marked otherwise, assume everything
you read is private and confidential.

This poem is private and confidential;
it cannot be thought about without the author's permission.

The poems before and after it are private and confidential;
seek legal advice before making any connections.

All poems have a right to a private life;
please be respectful of this, particularly in the evening.

Some poems may do things they regret;
remember it is a criminal offence to show compassion.

Take into account the poem's age at publication;
the poem may have been very different in composition.

Some poems are minors where tougher rules apply:
readers must complete mandatory training by a date that's passed.

While the law does not cover vulnerable poems,
guidelines are available on the intranet. To access them,

please use the login and password that were sent to you
during a period of illness. We regret that these cannot

be reissued if you deleted them because you were anxious;
contact your line manager stating full reasons for the loss.

It is a requirement for communications to be painfully honest
in order for the institution to be compliant with new regulations.

Of course, your disclosure is private and confidential
and cannot be passed on without your prior consent in writing.

We reserve the right to lie to you and laugh behind your back.
A whole team party will be held, wine and nibbles provided,

there will be party hats and those hooter things, someone from
IT will have Kool and the Gang's 'Celebration' on their phone.

A code of conduct must be signed before re-reading this poem.
No responsibility will be taken for any misunderstandings.

Drafts

Dear [insert wrong name here, preferably that of the person most likely to be offended],

Many thanks [for all the sex we had], [your body is] much appreciated.

Yes of course, happy to help [you start a riot], just let me know when [and where we can go ape shit].

All best for the summer [of '69, and all that implies, and Woodstock and the song by Bryan Adams and a whole sunny chorus of hippies 69-ing],

[Insert name and electronic signature]

DISCLAIMER
I don't mean any of this but there's a 0.01% chance you might think it if you hold this email up to the light and in my defence please know that 30 minutes have passed since I clicked on the 'New Message' panel and now I'm going to be late for my train and have to change twice at this time of day and I'll be feeling sick rewriting it all again in my head on platform 3 because I can't stop, can't stop, can't stop checking my email.

I agree to read all the terms and conditions

to the point of exhaustion: please, give me a thesis-length
volume of them, daily, add this to my list of duties and
do not compensate me for the extra hours, request that
all terms and conditions are printed in 8-point font and
recommend I purchase a customised magnifying glass
from a preferential online company which will involve
further terms and conditions to agree to in order to conduct
fair examination of the thesis-length vols. now accelerating
their rate of arrival to three times a day now in 6-point font.

I agree to carry out the necessary actions required in order to
complete the tick boxes at the end with professional integrity.
These include (i) successful completion of one undergraduate
law degree (ii) a postgraduate diploma in business and finance
(iii) psychiatric screening to assess capacity to make complex
decisions in a given timeframe (iv) certification as an instructor
in a sport or leisure pursuit for added breadth (v) acceptance for
additional borrowing to cover the costs of (i) to (iv) above and
(vi) new ability to lie about what I am doing with my time.

In agreeing to all terms and conditions, I understand that it is
my responsibility to ensure that (a) all possible nuances of
meaning are detected/held in my head for as long as I shall
live (b) there is no violation of obscure pieces of international
legislation past/present (c) the pavements are free from broken
glass, parents need never worry again (d) all those who have
swallowed batteries now unswallow them (e) people who can't
remember when they took their pills now remember with no
possibility of accidental overdose (f) every effort is made
not to cry in cafés/the office/in front of partner/child.

Poem on Checks

check your inbox	check you haven't sent porn	check where they've got to	check you haven't killed them	check you heard correctly
check you can't be sacked	check the bathroom's free	check it's your blood on the tampon	check it's them, not you	check it's not schizo-phrenia
check if it'll be sunny	check you can't go blind	check your bank balance	check they cannot sue you	check the pH levels
check you haven't drunk the bleach	check there's enough paper	check your letter isn't sexy	check the joint is properly cooked	check it isn't drugs
check your tax return before filing	check you've not committed fraud	check what time we're eating	check your pans for poison	check your breasts monthly
check it's not indecent exposure	check your chin for toothpaste	check you haven't slashed your throat	check the news online	check you've not brought down the government
check no one saw your PIN	check they can't pin it on you	check directions for use	check it can't get in your bloodstream	check with a doctor if symptoms persist
check it's not meningitis	check there's a seat spare	check it can't get up your arse	done?	check it all again

Pure O

O you sound oh so perfect!
O you pure heavenly new moisturiser on the market!
O you pure luxury liner, I can afford your sea-facing superior cabins!
O you pure amphetamine pill, joy for weekends in the city!
O you pure virgin in vanilla rewrite of a classic S&M story!
O you pure spanking newfound element, chemists climaxing as I type!
O, O, O psycho fisherman pure O pulling me in like a pike
Pissed-up pure O, fighting outside pubs in torn leathers
Pork pie hairdo pure O, always finding fault with the menu
Po-faced pure O, escalating the complaint to the manager
Principal examiner pure O, failing the whole year for doing drugs
Patriarchal discourse pure O, refusing seats for pregnant women
Pure O you perfect master bastard, not a mark or blemish on you

Avoidances

Contemporary Policemen in Their Homes

Contemporary policemen in their homes keep us from harm,
keep their razors zipped in freezer bags, do not touch door handles,
return to the scene of human waste witnessed by former officers,
forecast which rooms could be next, radio for back-up several years
in advance, live with the gut feeling that this room could be the one
where someone will snap unprovoked in full possession of their faculties
so there is no case for 'diminished responsibility' as the person suffers
daily with 'hyper-responsibility' once calling their therapist terrified
that they could cause a train accident because an innocent lemonade
can flipped from their bag onto the track and in their mind was seen
to vault unaided onto the rail to balance long enough to meet the
16.33 at speed, should they go to the station on a Sunday at dawn
and remove it and all other litter just to be sure?

Contemporary policemen in their homes confiscate journals
where the suspect has written motives for the above in code,
take into custody those titles that arouse suspicion, zip *White Bears
and Other Unwanted Thoughts* into another freezer bag to be held
in a secure location undisclosed to the next of kin who sleeps soundly
beside them every night unaware of the intelligence assigned to the glass
of water, the extra strong kind that has been known to perform violence
in films, contemporary policemen advise caution and inform residents
that all domestic water is drunk out of plastic beakers between the hours
of 10 and 6 and householders found breaking this curfew may be charged.
This beat is too much for contemporary policemen who wish for transfer
to the Traffic Division where, white-gloved like in Ladybird books, they
could finally be calm in their homes, not always be working.

Section 3: Details of Project

In no more than 400 words, please outline the full scope and rationale of your project, including aims, objectives, format, costings, schedule and expected outcomes.
The 'New Hands' project seeks to replace my biological hands with artificial ones. A key objective is to discover an artificial pair of hands that are detachable and durable, capable of being securely stored when not in use or travelling on public transport, as well as able to withstand repeated deep cleaning with minimal impact on my time and quality of life while limiting the frequency of social embarrassment. In order to accomplish this, the project will be undertaken in four phases. I will first investigate two areas: a) the different means of removing and disposing of my hands in a way that is ethical, safe and irreversible; b) the range of artificial hands globally available, with specific reference to size, colour, surface texture, flexibility, sensory capacity, processes of attachment, auto-clean function and price. Consideration will then be given to the comparable strengths and weaknesses of the options in the form of a 6,000–8,000 word essay. The essay, to be submitted to a peer-reviewed journal, will conclude with a list of recommendations. The third phase will comprise a piece of field work. Guided by the list of recommendations, I will further explore at least one way of removing and disposing of my biological hands (for example, a site visit to a textile cutting service) and at least one way of replacing them with an artificial pair (for example, a suite of interviews with specialist surgeons).

The fourth and final phase will be the production of a sequence of poems which will present the agony of this and admit the deep shame I feel about willing something so brutal upon myself where others have no choice. This sequence will form part of a poetry collection of sufficient thickness that it can be gripped by an international audience of others who are preparing for, or are already in possession of, a pair of artificial hands following mental torment. Preliminary research indicates that representation of this demographic in the genre has so far been limited, making this work timely.

Costs will include: full-time cover of my present post for a period of six months; office costs (e.g. electricity, heating, and computing) for five months; accommodation, travel and subsistence for the field work; and the emotional and domestic costs associated with an extensive period of rumination (e.g. midnight calls to helplines, private couple counselling, disrupted family mealtimes). A full breakdown can be provided upon request.

Day two of sick leave

and I go to the Komedia mid-morning to take my mind off
things, look for the red and white stripy can-can legs of the
exterior – so Ronald McDonald high jinks, so Wicked Witch
of the East low camp, *so Brighton* – and drift in with what
I assume are people in a better place than me, on a skive or
retired cheeky date or passing by and fancying it. We're here
to see *The Favourite*. I've heard the sex is good and it's just
so much fun. The people who tell me this don't know about
me but today I'm desperate. I ask for a large red like I'm at a
party and toast paid sick leave. The adverts start and one of
them is dangerous. The party sours. I knew this would happen.
The wine in the glass is screaming and I'm gripping the seat
like I'm on a crashing plane, plunging into a scene of ducks
and geese running amok. There are just too many animals,
people and countries to think about, so I slam up the seat
and flee through the exterior wall. Those are not fun legs,
they are a tribute to all who are trapped inside whose severed
legs ooze from the wreckage of their minds, their bodies last
seen soaring over the Palace Pier, their heads in their hands,
tightly-wound engines knowing this is how and where it ends.

Safety-seeking Behaviours

1. I collect volcanoes.
2. If we're drinking ammonia, I'll drink you under the table baby.
3. Hairdryer fallen into the bath? You'll be all right. I once showered and shampooed a 55" television and was totally fine.
4. I'll take you to the edge. Of the Grand Canyon. We'll see condors!
5. No, overalls slathered in varnish definitely WON'T blow up the washer-dryer if you miss out the wash cycle and set to dry-extra.
6. Worried that you have accidentally given your cat fabric conditioner? Stare at it. All day. With enough concentration, you will empty its gut of anything untoward, including the cup of coffee you probably gave it earlier.
7. I eat piranhas. Raw, with my head fully-immersed in the Amazon.
8. One more hand wash won't hurt; it's only boiling water from the kettle.
9. Spent matches in a clean, empty porcelain dish have the unique ability to reignite and set fire to your house – and your elderly neighbour's – but only if it's *you* who left them and you've just gone out.
10. I went private to have my windpipe taken out.
11. Concerned that the combi boiler has grown a new valve that is leaking an odourless, poisonous gas? Search for old pictures of you and your family that include the kitchen. Stare at them. Count and recount the valves. You might have to make allowances for the time of day, but you'll get inconclusive evidence for sure.
12. We have to take risks otherwise no one would ever get anything done. So yes, by all means, pipe bathroom sealant onto your toothbrush and ignore the taste.
13. I race ostriches. Barefooted, no headgear.

Discuss the Past Twelve Years with Reference to One US Soap Opera

Perhaps I should imagine they were a mistake
like when they killed off Bobby Ewing in *Dallas*
then brought him back again, turning around in
the shower to wish Pam *Good Morning*, telling
her that the whole series had been a dream,
he was alive (and okay!), alive (and okay!).

Perhaps I am Pam, no, Bobby, the past twelve years
my dead-not-really-dead years, a very long episode
in a big hot shower, that today I am so clean and
moisturised and ready to do a fuck-off business deal
with the world, that I was never in a coma in the desert
rooms of therapists, Pam outside in the car crying,

that I wake this morning knowing that no ring binders
exist with 'R. Ewing' on the spine, no hole-punched
A4 jotter notes with 'Bobby, Wednesday' in biro,
that they have evaporated like mist off a bathroom tile
and I will put on a plaid shirt and jeans too tight around
the crotch, sport a buckle as big as my cock and sock

a right hook into the jaw of JR in his office, desk piled
high with swatches of self-help books disguised as
business papers behind which he grins 'n' swivel chairs.
That was for suggesting it in the first place, buddy,
I will drawl before the camera cuts to me in bed with Pam,
clinking glasses, screen full of Bobby Ewing Joy,

no more drama, no more pain, the sun out, the air dry.

The Outsider

I live in a hide,
brain on the binocular hook,
lungs on the fold-down latch,
nerves on a ledge.

I see in slats,
planks grained with people,
dizzying parallelograms of traffic,
belt-straps of departing light.

No one knows I am here
but I have my breath
to blow cool glass scrolls,
maps for living in the mist.

Magical Thinking

Virginia Woolf Has Fallen Over

Virginia Woolf has fallen over and *this* means: someone will complain about me / the car that overtook us on the A23 at 10am last Sunday in clear conditions, skidded 90°, recovered and carried on will overtake us again but this time we won't be so lucky / the red nail varnish on the train table where I put my laptop this morning was not red nail varnish, it was contaminated blood / my throwaway comments in a café have been recorded / I have an undiagnosed heart condition / I have ingested dried superglue left on scissors used to cut open a finger of UHT milk subsequently poured into an unwanted coffee which, for the sake of good working relationships, I was compelled to accept and while I have now stood Virginia Woolf back up on the shelf, I can't remember which book she was originally in front of and *this* means: someone will make a complaint about my throwaway comments in a café / my heart will give way from the sight of a car skidding / we will skid, some of us will die and it will be because my lungs are superglued together / one of us will need a blood transfusion, but it will go wrong because they will use red nail varnish and I'm now stood in front of Virginia Woolf, staring, wondering what would happen if I turned her 90° to the right / painted her nails / superglued her feet to the MDF / would everything be okay? / would she complain?

My Stay in That Hotel Was Just Out of a Magazine

First, a full-page feature of a never-felt-better woman in summer issue hues: creamy teacup nesting in her hands like a chick, perched on a modern rocking chair upholstered in 'distressed turquoise'* looking out to sea through newly-cleaned balcony doors under a jaunty fuchsia roof of *What are you waiting for?* guttered by a *Get the life you want!* in egg yolk yellow *(*outlets and prices for cup, chair, pumps and Breton top detailed at the back)*;

second, a reduction in size for the COMPACT (HANDBAG) VERSION now sharing ¼ of the page with an ad for a lift that comes down into your living room which you step out of laughing, restaurant-dressed, hair done and definitely not lonely as you walk towards a blurred-out seated figure who is ready to go, you who said it was important that the never-felt-better woman went on her own to get the life she wanted and ***LOOK INSIDE!*** she still has her teacup, modern rocking chair, *What are you waiting for?* and full list of stockists even though now there's bird shit dripping like egg white down one of the balcony doors;

next to go is the modern rocking chair and the half-smile because now she is standing with sciatica and now they have your money, you've been through the whole magazine, eaten the four complimentary Celebrations, and it never takes long as there's nothing in it and the magazine has that character of unwanted fancy chocolate opened then left in the fridge and both she and you are left wondering *What are we waiting for?*

until a month, maybe two, have gone by and while the next issue is out it has not been bought for there is a feeling that one is not so desperate and so the woman in the marina hotel lives on in the house but now her world has been shoved into a magazine pile in the corner of the lounge which the cat has sprayed up and some plastic tat from a fast food place lies on the top and deters you from rifling for the magazine because you'd have to hold the plastic tat for another few seconds, relive the day that you didn't plan for lunch, shouted at your partner then took everyone to the retail park to eat that crap which at first felt good, then felt awful, especially when you bought your order again because the first one wasn't enough;

but if you were to retrieve the magazine and turn to this page you would find that the feature has changed drastically – gone are the pumps and the Breton top, the never-felt-better woman has been recycled into *When loved ones need us most* and it's hard to tell what exactly she is going through because they've cut her down to a head held in hands so it could be a breakdown, there's a ring of black polo neck so it could be a bereavement, there's a fuzzy outline of someone standing in the same white studio space so it could be divorce, they've deliberately left it open to interpretation and it's clear that the woman is in crisis, not having a good time or making the most of what she paid £163 for even if there is breakfast included and the option of late checkout for she is no good

on her own, her imagination running wild, calling up Reception to remove the property of the previous guests: first a CHANEL bag of used hand soaps which she thought contained cocaine for how else was she to account for the white dust she saw earlier on the black coffee table which she had to move to the corner of the room so that she would not breathe it in or, worse, touch it when she set down her teacup and be implicated in someone else's illegal activities against her will; then a stash of tissue paper shoe inserts kicked under the bed by cocaine dealers in new boots who had disposed of the soaps they had used to wash their hands after an orgy in her room but were not so careful and had tripped over teacups and modern rocking chairs on the way out and spilt their drugs and this is what my stay in that hotel was like, it was just out of a magazine, it was not what I was waiting for, it was not the life I wanted.

System Administrator

flashes up in the middle of writing poems

System Administrator seeks permission to launch Wizard Doctor

System Administrator has encountered a problem, click here to read report

System Administrator finds that you are an international pervert

System Administrator is installing update 1 of 3,
please do not turn off your machine

System Administrator is reporting you to Interpol

System Administrator is installing update 2 of 3,
please remain in your seat

System Administrator thinks you do not deserve to love or be loved

System Administrator is installing update 3 of 3,
please do not jump out of the window

System Administrator says they should bring back hanging
for the likes of you

System Administrator requests read receipt

System Administrator knows you're lying on the bed
with the curtains closed

System Administrator sees you grip your head like it's a nut,
your hands the spanner

System Administrator is not your mother,
but how funny would it be if it was?

System Administrator advises immediate restart

System Administrator is waiting

System Administrator is waiting

After being unable to tell the Samaritans

I tell you how the thoughts have changed,
how they can now come out of walls,

how they work this gaffer tape, this rope,
how there's no ransom note, no recording,

no concrete floor and no single light bulb,
how it's happening right here, how I am

drinking this pint with a knife to my throat,
how *I just can't say ... but ... you know.*

We escape the pub to snowfall. Talk.
Leave two sets of tracks on the path.

PhD Viva

1.1 Arrival

I already knew I'd have to take the truck, but didn't reckon on the truck having ideas of its own, flying off the ferry ramps at Dover, jamming the accelerator pedal, the speedometer rising up and up and up, police cars swerving, pedestrians diving out of the way like grotesque dolphins, up the A3, bending round the M25, up the M1 going north like Frankenstein, *mush mush* my brain went as the husky grey road shrank from three lanes to two to one small country road in Scotland, *mush mush* until there was nowhere left to go but through the bent red NO ENTRY sign, along the private jetty into Loch Ness where the waters were black and deep, in we went, my truck, my *mush mush*, my pack of huskies, me in bloodied furs, mad eye gleaming, hell-bent on getting that truck *somewhere* out of *there*, NOW in Loch Ness, no wonder people's brains are tricked into seeing images of monsters, here's a runaway truck with husky dogs and a bandaged mental patient driver shaking his fist at the windscreen as ACADEMIC NIGHTMARE LOGISTICS plunges into the depths like a great white whale.

1.2 Warm-up questions

I was both the demon driver obsessed with the bends *and* the tourists on shore buying Nessie T-shirts, my examiners the boat tour captains *and* the ice-lolly-licking parents supervising their kids climbing the Nessie slide in the dinky playground outside the Nessie shop and they are smiling through all of it, telling me I have passed but to hell with all that, *what the fuck is going on?* I am battling with the seatbelt, my foot trapped under the clutch, my mind flipping through the memory of a Christmas stocking survival manual past the quicksand and snakebite sections *where the fuck is it?* I scream inside NOW locating the diagram of a drowning car the need to 'allow the vehicle to be fully immersed before attempting the door so that the air pressure either side is equal' *(have you the reference?)* and then I am the inky figure leaking out of the descending truck and being sucked up to the top of the page

1.3 A cosy chat

into an Italian restaurant to celebrate and my supervisor is there and my examiners are eating spaghetti and I notice that my shoes are tangled in black reeds like rotten bandages and I am wondering whether the huskies made it too when I see a truck tyre roll across the floor from the gents to the bar, then another, then another, and my supervisor asks why they have to decorate the place with number plates and I am alarmed to recognise one of them and something is lurking in the depths, something is starting up again, all the tables NOW have wing mirrors and my examiners are checking their chins for tomato sauce and then the waiter arrives with an oversize plate bearing a steaming engine and I have no idea how to eat it and here's the waiter again, asking if I would like a little oil, all the menus are bending, the napkins turning to mush, and a man in a wolf jacket is telling me I dropped something at the bar, is handing me these cold, wet keys.

Today You Went to Lunch with a Cave

It wasn't the first time, so your eyes
didn't widen when it arrived, trying
the door first frontwards, then side-on
like an overgrown shore crab.

The waiter took its shabby
medieval cart as the cave sloped
into its seat, spreading its grey
slabs around like dusty skirts.

The table next to you stared
deep into the cave's mouth;
it performed a polite smile of
rock and lichen, debris breaking

at the corners like torn bread.
You asked the cave how it was,
talked about the weather, what
a nightmare the bus was, but

there was no echo and you wondered
if you had got the right cave. You
lobbed in more words, some sharp
as flint, others smooth as shale,

and you heard, in the distance, contact
with water, the sound of weighted
objects, plummeting, and you knew
that this was your cave all right,

the cave you drifted into one
spring day on a Cornish beach
and buried secrets in disturbed sands,
the cave which, over the years,

gave you shelter, adventure, whose
fissures grew like cracking ice,
whose darkness was washed darker
by restless tides until there were

overcast days like these where
the cave came to you and you couldn't
tell whether it was finally still
or just a wave away from collapse.

Thought-Action-Fusion

Fear Brain

Fear Brain has no respect for Monday mornings and remote access.
Fear Brain and its knuckle duster say *Let's go out and wreck stuff!*
Fear Brain takes a baseball bat to standard messages, bulldozes
calendars, beats to a pulp the sticky notes they rocked up with.
Fear Brain opens all attachments in Junk with a flick knife,
drives a stolen car into shared files, hunts down individuals
in this document, hits 'replace all' with 'bollocks, the lot of it'.
Fear Brain and its gang of hoodlums break and enter hotels
of incorrect data, punch SUBMIT NOW, send it flying through
windows, douse laptops and all devices on this network in petrol,
set them alight with the BBQ ignitor since you're WFH, so WTF?
Fear Brain pisses in your first coffee, pisses its jeans laughing,
doesn't change, hasn't changed since it last aggravated mobs of
prehistoric lizards to scarper, save their precious signet ring skins.

Prefrontal Cortex

Prefrontal Cortex would like to invite you to a day of reflection.
Prefrontal Cortex says places are limited, please bring vegetarian lunch.
Prefrontal Cortex is faffing with a flipchart.
Prefrontal Cortex says *imagine you are a piece of fruit.*
Prefrontal Cortex tells you it is a greengage before announcing it studied at Oxbridge.
Prefrontal Cortex is vague about subject, qualification and length of study.
Prefrontal Cortex is more comfortable on a cushion on the floor.
Prefrontal Cortex says *you are welcome to sit in a chair if that is easier for you.*
Prefrontal Cortex puts a cushion under your feet while everyone stares at you in a chair.
Prefrontal Cortex is in its 40s and lives in a housing co-operative.
Prefrontal Cortex is proud of its anti-capitalist stance.
Prefrontal Cortex has a problem with car drivers.
Prefrontal Cortex has never had its bike nicked because it got it off Freecycle.
Prefrontal Cortex has a girlfriend, not a partner, and says so as much as possible.
Prefrontal Cortex has not always been doing this.
A long time ago Prefrontal Cortex had a career in accountancy.
Prefrontal Cortex tells you it got its clothes for daily practice from a charity shop.
Prefrontal Cortex did not see you when it was in Next last weekend with its girlfriend.
Prefrontal Cortex has brought a bag of biros for the next exercise.
Prefrontal Cortex would like them all back by the end.
Prefrontal Cortex only recently got a mobile phone.
Prefrontal Cortex says it doesn't know how to use it and might donate it to Africa.
Prefrontal Cortex requests that evaluations are placed face down next to it as you leave.
Prefrontal Cortex sees immediately you've given the course a 3.
Prefrontal Cortex is imagining you as a bag of satsumas on the floor.
Prefrontal Cortex picks up the chair you sat in and raises it to a great height before stacking.

Prefrontal Cortex is unlocking its bicycle from the lamppost beside your lease car.

Prefrontal Cortex has the bag of biros in its pocket, not all reunited with lids.

Prefrontal Cortex bends sufficiently for a nib to make contact with the car's paintwork.

Prefrontal Cortex does everything slowly, with purpose and a sense of curiosity.

Prefrontal Cortex sods off down the street on its bike, screams *accept what is as what is.*

Think of it in Terms of Geometry

On good days
I am mistaken
for an isosceles triangle,

balanced enough
to fit into
human patterns

of backgammon boards,
boat sails,
the hands of a clock

and this would be fine
if it wasn't
for the angles,

amending my surface
area with
their expansions

and contractions
of papery
doubt.

It's hard work
holding three sides
at once,

maintaining
a tent
of composure,

flapping
bunting on cold,
lightless days

against
the sure
dial of protractors.

The Other Side of the Quarter Panel Mirror

It had crossed her mind how

I look in the mirror
the facial hair
my moustache

this central defender's build
the body I buy men's clothes for
no *hormonal imbalance, take metformin*

My mind is blown
the reluctance to look at people
being in groups, a team at work even, yet

I used to think
how companionable I was, if not good-looking
kicked like a football by my previous owners

Yet we both know
I haven't responded well to training
can only sit long enough for treats before
a furry cloud fallen to the ground

I could be a bison, I've grazed their plains

It explains everything
how in biology I'm a ruminant

I could be a buffalo.

the signs are there:
a velvety snout,
a tuft damp with nostril juice;

all shoulders, no hips, thin legs,
the shape of a map of America,
just features natural to buffalos.

it now makes sense:
the endless walking for I don't know what,
saying nothing, neck lowered to grass.

I was once probably a dog:
a cleaned-up, rescued mongrel,
lovable, now, to a kind woman.

there's no canine in me:
in all our time together,
I balloon into brown,
too heavy to stay up.

but more accurately I'm a buffalo.

the public comedy of my looks,
how in fear I might stampede.

HELP WALLY!

Wally's feelings are in a mess! Psychologists say that he did not develop enough cortisol receptors in infancy which affects his ability to cope with stress. Help Wally sort out his latest tangle. Draw lines to match the correct response to each external event. The first one has been done for you.

the spotting of an error
in the paperwork

dolphin sighting

the witnessing of the spontaneous
combustion of a great aunt

encounter on a dark moorland
with a headless horseman

approval for promotion

visit by carriage, with top hat
and cane, to local lunatic asylum

refusal of any further lending
by the bank

sudden oozing of ectoplasm from
dining room lampshade

letter from mystery benefactor
conferring vast fortune

sound of angels singing
from a boarded-up attic room

acute dizziness and impulse to
vomit

mental image: the apocalypse, the
world alight in flame

uncontainable joy

mild irritation and resolution to
make a phonecall

mental image: public outcry,
home destroyed by frenzied mob

desire to chant obscenities
whilst performing folksy jig

unpleasant sensation in lower body,
as if legs are about to give way

mental note to report activity
at the next meeting of the parish council

immediate need to empty bowels

urge to strangle every
last one of the bastards

Newly in love, distracted neuroscientists ♥

neurogenesis ♥ new neural pathways ♥ noticing how consciousness can change even in an adult mouse learning its way around a maze for food ♥ Neapolitan ice cream ♥ noticing how ice creams can spontaneously grow new flavours ♥ pistachio Nerf guns ♥ quivering lips then b-b-b-ANG! ♥ going nuts ♥ being so crazy 4 _____ + not noticing how some poor fucker has been triggered ♥ dreaming up new neural pathways ♥ Neanderthals + their unnoticed nighties ♥ plasticity ♥ particularly not noticing how some poor fucker's consciousness is tangled in plastic bags like endangered turtle stomachs ♥ nature ♥ noticing how plants can trigger thoughts of chemical production in response to external force ♥ new branches in brain science ♥ neuroscientists + plasticity sitting in a tree ♥ K-I-S-S-I-N-G ♥ ignoring the tree, the poor fucker, thinking of how it can be relieved of the new weight ♥ singin' 'Chapel of Love' like they're the new Dixie Cups ♥ unique New York honeymoons ♥ melting ♥ thinking *this is it* ♥ not giving a fuck about trees + mice + turtles + Neanderthal nightmares thinking *this really is it I'm dying.*

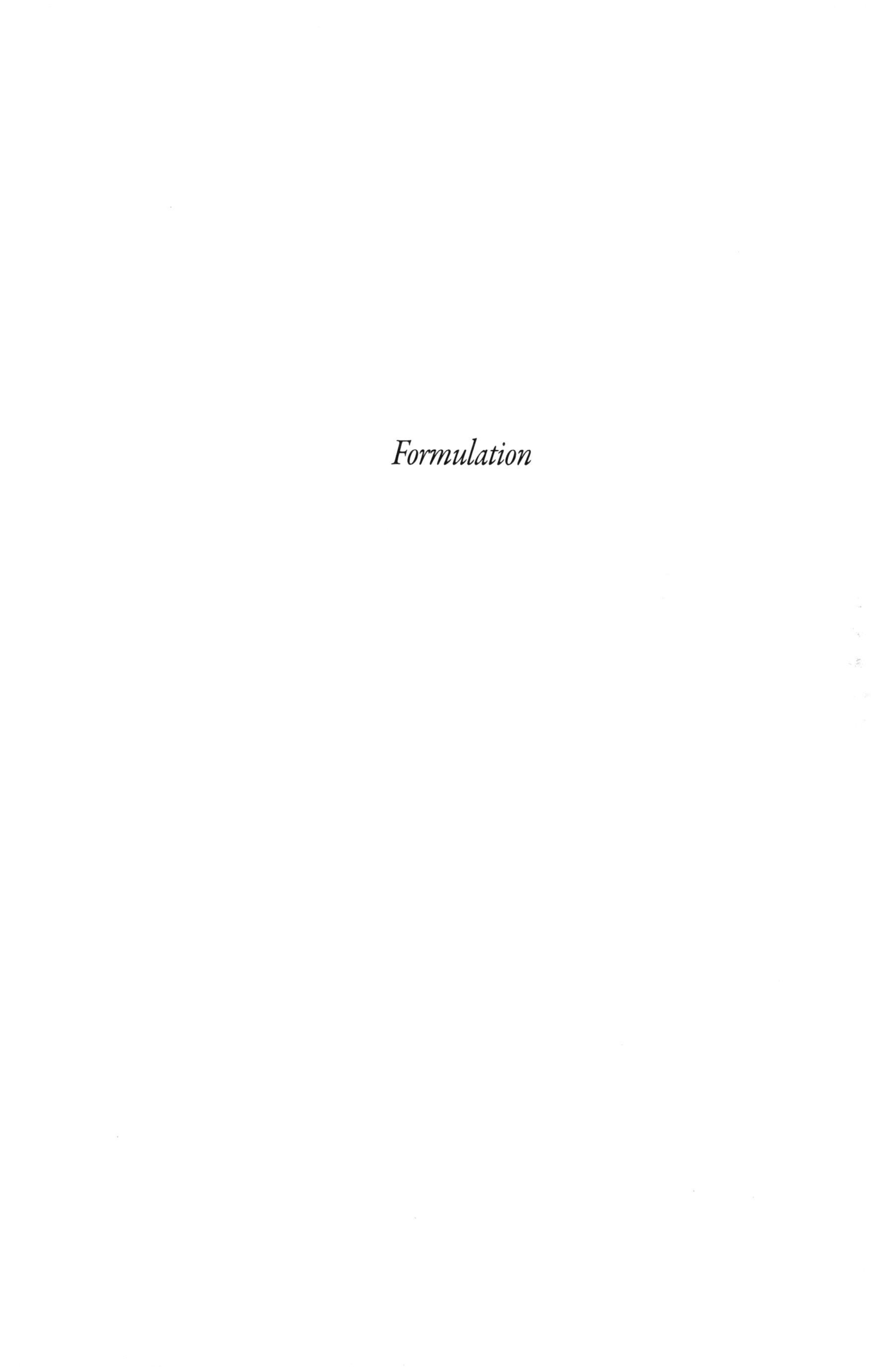

Formulation

I Prefer to Get My Information from Unreliable Sources

I am a heart surgeon.
I eschew medical school and additional training
in a subspecialised area
for a game of Operation.
Don't bother me with talk of stents and ventricles
on theatre days – play a few rounds with me!
If I can ease out all the pieces without touching the sides
then all patients on today's list will live.
It's useful revision of human biology, too;
I've removed a few white buckets from knees in my time.

I am an astronaut.
I eschew space agency advanced training
with language component
for trade catalogues.
When they do a shot from inside the Soyuz on launch day,
that's not a manual I'm consulting, specifying
all possible malfunctions and their solutions
as your reporter explains back in the studio;
it's an old issue of *Plumbing and Heating Supplies*.
Cognitively demanding work, looking for budget mixer taps;
takes the edge off, all that space given to choices in chrome.

I am a footballer.
I eschew my bodily instincts
for what other customers
who bought this item are reading.
When a cross comes in I try to leave it long enough to nip off
pitch, grab my holdall and, in the quiet of
the changing room, sprint down the index of a book
with long title and even longer subtitle in imperatives, see if
the exact angle of the cross is listed and, if so, some strategies
for tackling it. It never is, but I feel better for checking.
I'm at the top of my game, focus-wise, pundits say.

We Have Made a Number of Key Appointments

So, it's agreed: you're to go round licking toilet seats.
The Area Manager has done the rota, set the targets.
This week you're on public toilets, West Sussex.
Can you lick twenty in Worthing, fifteen in Chichester?

Any chance your tongue might stretch to Hampshire?
Portsmouth Harbour is understaffed; it would be good
experience. You can manage your own diary: lick seats
Monday to Friday, or lick all thirty-five on a Tuesday

morning if you want, though you have to take into
account the A27 on a weekday. Don't forget:
most councils operate a summer and winter timetable
and some facilities are closed at Christmas and New Year.

It's advisable to take a stash of 20ps: you can claim
these back as expenses. The goal is to lick toilet seats
whenever the opportunity arises, not to pick and choose:
lick 'em in McDonald's, lick 'em in John Lewis.

Ignore the Cleaning Supervisor's log by the entrance;
look at that and you're getting into checking again,
and besides, it's unreliable evidence; we all know
that '9ams' are initialled and ticked off at 8.

Don't loiter beforehand; that's looking for trouble.
You cannot tell how clean a toilet seat is by looking
at who just left the cubicle, if they have piercings
or plasters, how well they wash their hands, and

don't walk the length of the place prodding saloon doors
like you're inspecting a defrosted chicken; you've got to
make a decision and stick to it, cut down on all the time
spent planning and reviewing and get on with your day.

The Area Manager will be available by phone or Skype
if you need any help, and yes she's done it herself, lots
of times, although she draws a line at kitchen counters.
This is a permanent position with an immediate start.

Theory A, Theory B

Theory A:
the therapist has sketched a diagram of how

creates a cycle

Theory B:
daydreaming of better times, the therapist has drawn a picture of a fantasy bicycle

Evidence:
a series of swooping lines, uneven boxes and different-sized circles denoting three hundred thoughts per minute has been blue-biroed into my notebook

Evidence:
look at the ridiculous size of those wheels, the peculiar, plunging crossbar, the spongy seat manufactured by a T. H. Reat & Company, why ... it's a penny-farthing!

Theory A:
the therapist has drawn this to illustrate the point being made

Theory B:
she's done it for her own amusement, so many years have passed blah blahing on about this stupid problem, wouldn't you do something similar if you were her?

Evidence:
the lines and circles have been tapped with the pen and the BIGGEST circle with all the spokes is the one which I'm supposed to try, in future, to park – *park the thought and let it go*

Evidence:
she's come today in school ma'am costume with a Victorian countenance – sober, stately, staring ahead – towering over impossible stockings manufactured just for this occasion, the riding of the new and fantastic penny-farthing! She ain't going to park it anywhere guv'nor, she's off to Regent's Park

where wealthy families will stroll after Christmas feasts and jellies the shape of Bavarian castles and they'll point at the spectacle with bespoke walking sticks, the children in bonnets air-drawing the loony large wheel with spit as the Victorian schoolmistress lurches by licking her lips after Black Forest gâteau

Theory A:
the therapist has finished the explanation and I am being invited to reflect

Evidence:
the notebook has been handed back to me and the therapist has gone silent and after what feels like two thousand years something is said about the 'septicaemia' incident in a Pompeii garden something about how *intrusive thoughts are rarely about the real cause of the anxiety* something is said about guilt and shame something is said about the core beliefs that drive us and how they are the small but powerful component of a thought which is the much bigger circle like a wheel but it's the small wheel we need to pay attention to *what is it that's behind all this is it that you think you're a bad person is it that you think you ought to be punished with fifty lashes of the birch?*

Theory B:
the penny-farthing festive hullaballoo has come to its natural close

Evidence:
the wealthy families have returned to their houses in Belgravia and the governess has been kindly escorted to her lodgings to prepare her lessons and the amphitheatrical velocipede has been parked where it is covered in a protective cloth and on the cloth are the initials of the manufacturer and the initials are exactly the same as mine they stand for Septimus Julius Magnus Brain S.J.M. Brain for short and *we'll do extra Latin next time when you might be ready to take more of this in*

The next poem

is based on a survey of 241 college students, probably American, probably living in the '80s, mostly and inexplicably female and there's a reasonable chance that the survey was conducted not by funded professionals or grad students but by a Psych major in a panic about their mid-term project and who knows how stoned the subjects were prior to the survey and how honest were they anyway and how relevant is this to me because my problems did not start until I was in my 30s but then I'm not being honest either because if I think about it properly – and we all know I am skilled in going over and over things until I reach a feeling of surety and/or exactitude – my earliest, persistent intrusive thought came when I was about 9 and told me that to ward off the possibility of re-enactment of *The Amityville Horror* – which my caregivers had rented on VHS from the garage instead of *Herbie Goes Bananas* – in the home, I would have to touch everything in my box room in a specified order from the confines of my bed after lights out and if I got it wrong I had to start over and if I got it right then another thought would tell me to do it again, two more times to round it up to three, and sometimes I would knock an object slightly or, worse, knock it off its shelf or, even worse, fall out of bed stretching and these were incidents that needed compensating for in an increased number of rounds if I was to avoid being slaughtered in the middle of the night by a handsome devil-possessed East Coast youth who probably wrote this survey the night before his paper was due in and haunted the dorm block in search of willing participants in exchange for dope:

The Thoughts **item (in jazzy font)**	experienced in the past 12 months	distress level (mark out of 10)
driving into a window while choking family member		
swearing in public while kissing authority figure		
sex with authority figure while removing dust from unseen places		
home unlocked, intruder there while catching sexually transmitted disease		
fly/blouse undone in front of authority figure who is choking family member		
driving authority figure into a window with fly/blouse undone ready to catch a sexually transmitted disease		
sex with window while removing dust blown up by authority figure when driven into window swearing		
hitting animals or people with car while removing all dust from floor		
disgusting sex act involving windows		
taps left on, home flooded by disgusted authority figure		
holding up bank to pay for repair of scratched car paint caused by hitting animals or people with car		
grabbing money from naked strangers in bank		
catching sexually transmitted disease from money		
naked authority figure hitting animals or people with getaway car		
sex in public with authority figure in dust-free car		
car unlocked, intruder there grabbing money while authority figure has additional sex with window		
disgusted naked strangers swearing in public, breaking window and hitting people having sex in dust-free cars while removing unseen money from unseen places		
authority figure choking naked strangers		
kissing authority figure while holding up second bank with fly/blouse undone in front of disgusting windows covered in dust and sexually transmitted diseases		

My Illness as a Collection of Ladders

It started out as a normal life event: buy a flat, buy a ladder,
don't think about the ladder at any other time except when it is needed;
acclimatise to the clatter of the ladder and feel no concern when the ladder starts
wearing an atlas of paint, poles crowned in emulsion, capital cities draped in gloss;
wonder at the sight of the ladder and its continuous ability to assist with tasks.
These are the ladders we are expected to have.

The second ladder came in a dream: I discovered
that ladders could have personalities, make choices about their appearance.
This one was not nice. Stocky, unshaven, it had evidently been carted around
on a builder's truck enough times to convincingly feature as an extra on *Bergerac*
playing the ladder that is just put away when the suspect realises he's been rumbled,
hurls his tools into the back and speeds off with a glance to camera.
This was a ladder I did not want to have.

That ladder came on holiday to Spain: passing undetected
through the scanners, it was unable to take a seat on the plane but clung on
in the hold, applying its upright-at-an-angle skills to take-off and the climb. It soon found
its articulated non-slip rubber feet at Malaga airport and ruined that holiday – ladders are not
designed to visit mountaintop seafood restaurants, get in Spanish taxis, have sex
in airless rooms, however expert their grip on variable ground.
This ladder was just out of shot in the photos.

Two ladders don't make a collection: but a concern
so disconcerting that I took Spanish holiday ladder to see a specialist,
asked if she had seen one like it, where I should keep it, when to use it. She said yes,
she's seen *lots of paintbrushes* before, for a long time she's been seeing a client with a
tradesman's multipack of them that have a nasty habit of turning up before big meetings –
the thing to do is to examine your childhood memories of paintbrushes.
Spanish holiday ladder and I paid £40 and left with a tester pot.

After that Spanish holiday ladder went everywhere: in my mind
I became skilled at accommodating it, ensuring its comfort with space to extend.
Before big meetings I would greet whoever was there, then look for a free corner. I put
it up in supermarkets, swimming pools, lugged it to hotels, family gatherings, observed all
public holidays, decorated it with the Christmas tree. It was heavy and could really hurt,
catching my fingertips, bashing my shins. I had permanent shoulder strain.
Spanish holiday ladder said we were good together.

Other ladders tried their luck: seeking rest and recuperation,
I took them in. I leant window cleaners' ladders out back, parked mobile safety steps
on the drive, stacked multipurpose folding ladders with the sheets and towels. Some ladders
I knew to be harmless, such as those out of magazines reconstituted to become bookshelves,
pot plant and photo frame for illustration purposes only. One was as small and slim as a
comb, a hamster's or from a child's playset maybe – but in a pocket, the meanest of all!
This little ladder dug in constantly.

My life was soon full of ladders: there was so much hidden
ladder admin, online order forms, confirmation emails, *Sorry we missed you*
cards as neighbours took in home deliveries while I was at work. At work they put ladders
in my pigeonhole, ladders took the Tube to see me in my office, ladders invited me to annual
meetings/forums/symposia/away days/reviews/one day special events, chaired them, minuted
them, asked me if I had any further thoughts and to let them know by a **date in bold**.
I did have further thoughts and they were about ladders.

I completed a questionnaire about ladders: yes they were interfering
with my life on a daily basis, yes I was finding it hard to derive enjoyment from the things
that once gave me pleasure and yes the quality of my relationships had been affected (see ■).
■ It is hard to a) get out of the door in the morning b) compete in sports and c) pay attention
to your partner while you are project managing a collection of ladders. I couldn't do the
further exercises in the book that would, *we GUARANTEE*, eliminate the problem.

There was a huge mountain to climb: in my home environment
I became stuck between the distinctive aluminium and wood formations of Mt. Ladder.
There was no give, not even for the *Sorry we missed you* cards which began to mount up
on the other side of the door so prominently the locals affectionately nicknamed it 'Post Hill'.
My days were all ladder, ladder, ladder, so bad I thought I would become a fossil. Future
civilisations would excavate broken finger bones, cracked shoulder blades.
I would be the first of The Ladder People.

Archaeologists would write speculative papers: how had I got there?
Hour long specials would be televised on a Sunday investigating my mysteries,
reconstructions of my life made on limited budgets with few actors, too much voiceover,
appalling audio (drums every time I ran, wheezing violins for emotional scenes). I would be
an Age of Globalisation sacrifice, a layer of burial ground, a victim of a volcanic eruption.
In casts of my jawline some would think they saw a scream.

No one would conclude it was ladders: in the contemporary moment
not even someone close who had also lived with ladders guessed that there was a problem
to do with ladders, who had gone on to have children who had started collections of ladders,
who phoned when I could still move my right arm to tell me that she was on the cancer ward,
who wanted me to visit, it had been a long time since I had visited, *please visit*.
I was too ashamed to mention ladders.

I couldn't leave the ladders: I tried to get expensive professional help
but by now I only had access to the inside of me – no good if you need to put on shoes,
lock the door, get in the car. A research fellow in phonetics will tell you that it is possible
to form sounds through the vocal cords alone, requiring no movement of the lips. Pressed
against ladders I managed /h/ as in '<u>h</u>elp', but no more, not even /m/ as in '<u>m</u>e' or '<u>m</u>um'.
It was not a scream. It was the beginning of a phrase I could not say.

Thoughts are not facts

are not the makeup you applied mid-session

not the wrong appointment time blamed on me

nor your boasts about shoplifting *just last week*

are not the clients who texted you while I cried

nor the replies you sent back as I bit my lip

not the years I spent funding your timeshare

not the fear I had of reporting you, of you reporting me

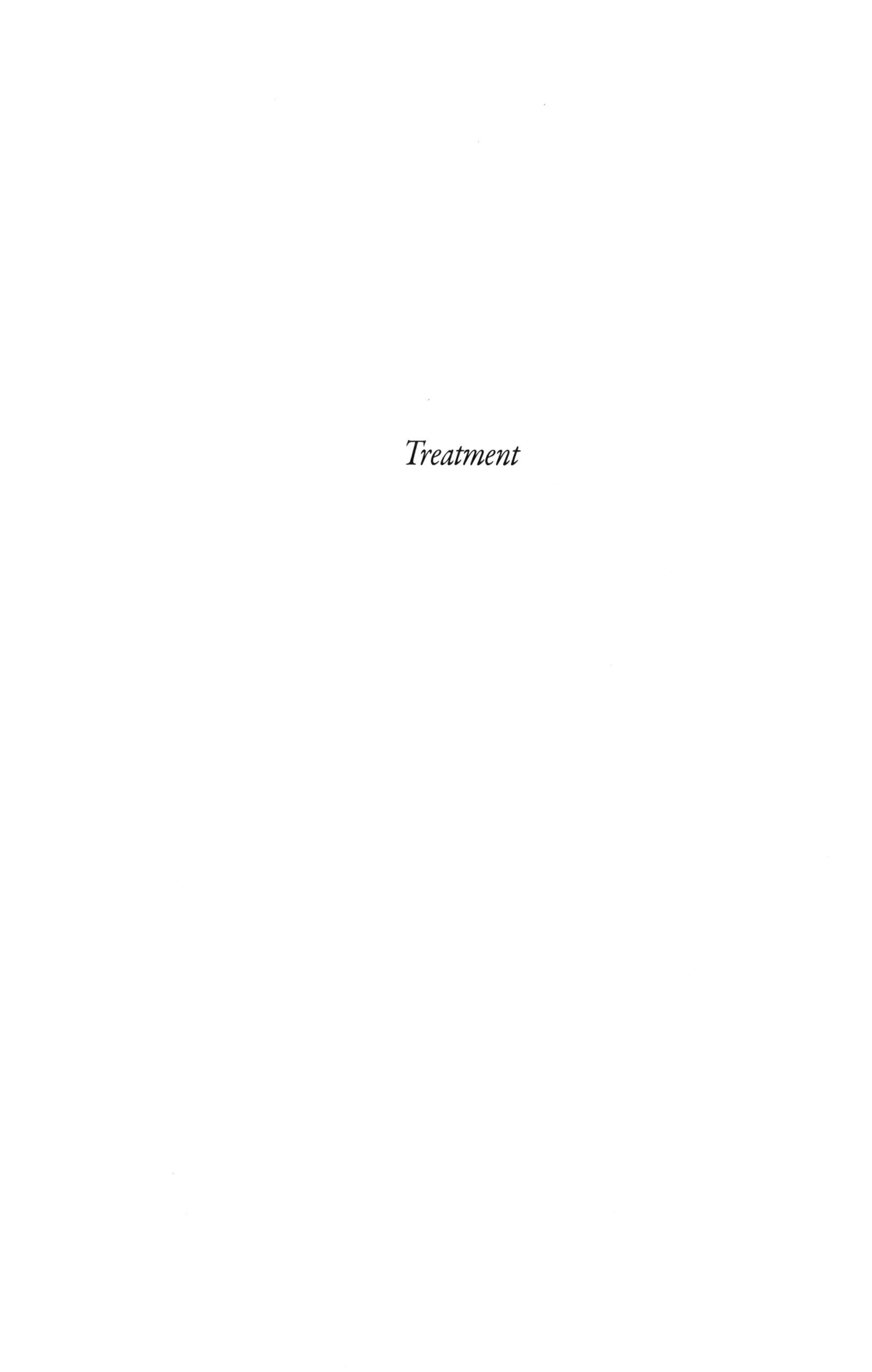

Treatment

2/17

Exposure

Second session in and we're looking up filth
on the internet

Response

clicking
on, then off

Prevention

a Tory MP, who comes
up first.

3/17

~~Exposure~~

It's not safe to expose ourselves
this afternoon –

a graph is drawn and I'm X'd
into the 90–100% zone.

We're to wait for the medication
to kick in, the levels to drop

and, meanwhile,
disrupt rumination time.

I'm given banners, whistles,
a Spider-Man costume.

Gonna abseil
down that graph,

demand my human rights,
break back into the world.

5/17

Exposure

We're back online; this time I face doing it
on my phone.

I read of all the ways I could murder
my lovers,

Response

trust this is the way forward:

Prevention

serial killers are my friends.

7/17

Exposure

The sun's out again and we joke
how I bring it with me.

But today we're bringing on the darkness.
Today I'm to sit in the pitch black and

Response

stare at his face,
stare into the face of Satan from

Prevention

that day up Devil's Dyke –

the engine revs,
what could but did not happen.

9/17

Exposure

I'm a careless, whispering pervert
shouting it

onto a piece of paper along
with all my other secret identities:

fraudster, perjurer,
kung-fu master,

closet case, basket case,
case-closed Elvis,

moon-landing faker,
moonin' fuckin' Moonraker.

Response

Give the piece of paper
to the police,

Prevention

give it
to the thought police.

11/17

Exposure

We're on to texting
chat up lines,

sexting
my Contacts list,

Response

not correcting
autocorrect,

welcoming 'thighs'
in place of 'thoughs',

gyrating greasy frisky frigging finger-lickin' thighs
of being

Prevention

a great big chicken.

13/17

Exposure

Licking toilet seats is so passé.
We're going to eat our dinner off 'em,

Response

make an occasion of it,
dress up, use knives,

forks, soup spoons,
and not shout *bastards!*

at your therapist and partner
when they go first –

Prevention

all that piss,
all that pent-up, steamed-up piss.

16/17

Subjective Units of Distress

0 it's been 6 weeks! We are ecstatic
to see each other

10 discover we holidayed in the same place
on different days

20 (no chance of a casual sighting
followed by coffee)

30 she forgets – for the first time in sixteen sessions –
to offer me water

40 lets me talk over her

50 something is up

60 I talk faster

70 something is wrong

80 I talk about endings, if it has to be done
then what my preferences are

90 she tells me she's leaving

100 the parallel universe where we end up kissing
explodes

17/17

THOUGHTS
we're finishing
I'll miss the wristwatch

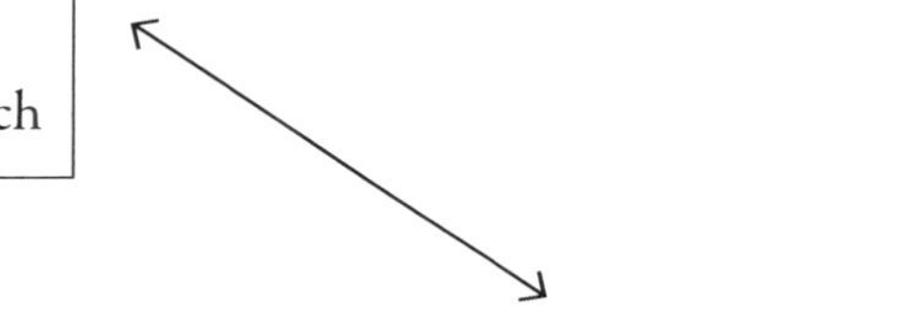

PHYSIOLOGICAL SENSATIONS
sting of arrows chucked into hearts chucking
out time following directions out to waiting
rooms chucking stinging hearts choking out
rings of chairs in waiting rooms on which are
sat some hearts checking the clocks checking
our watches ringing numbers on questionnaires
circling our pain choking on it going over and
over it going around ringing out *love makes
the world go round* filling out end-of-treatment
forms choking on hearts on surprise goodbye
handshakes making the world go round goatee
landlords pulling last pints watching chained-
up bikes unlock sunny afternoons swinging
down towpaths desire lines corridors receptions
past people in pet shops locksmiths artisan
bakeries ordering iced coffees sitting inside
keeping my shades on crying like all the babies
clocking my hands my tiny wonderful hands
holding on holding on to me holding on to her
pulling on heart-shaped watches crying choking
stinging thanking going

BEHAVIOURS
cycling through the agenda
not looking at her because my eyes are filling like locks
laughing about petting goats
not looking at her because canals are filling my throat
laughing about wasps down tops
not looking at her because my ears are ringing with pubs
drawing pendulums in swing
not looking at her because my heart is filling with clocks
adding all these arrows
not looking at her because the clocks are growing hands
handing over my thank you cards
not looking at her because I think my heart will stop

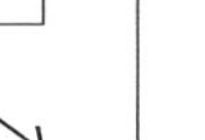

FEELINGS
sadness
awe
pride
love

Epilogue

Imaginal Exposure Story

I'm now over my OCD and as part of this I no longer do compulsions. One day the phone rings and it's *her*. She tells me she has a space at 3 or 4 later today, would I like to come? I admit that I would, but will have to cancel my other arrangements. She says she's *here* and *not going anywhere*. I send some texts without checking for mistakes and ten minutes later I'm getting back to her. *I AM free*, I tell her *Great*, she replies. We agree on 3.

Examples

A man who thought he'd written 'CUNT'
in each job application after pressing SEND.

A motorist who thought she'd run over every cyclist
she'd ever passed.

An office worker who thought he'd blow up the building
if he switched on the lights.

A business consultant who carried handcuffs to stop herself from
strangling the public.

A writer who thought they'd go to prison for everything
they said, did or wrote.

We are examples of people.

We are for instances, case studies, 'e.g.'s, *there was once*...s.

We live in boxes, full-page tables, flowcharts of the process
that keeps the problem going.

We open chapters then rescue readers from the boring bits later.

We are bold, ***we are bold italics***, we are first names only,
we are **names have been changed.*

We are intelligent, successful, work hard, love our families,
have hobbies and pets.

We are pilots, lorry drivers, lawyers, firefighters, artists, opticians,
we are managers in retail.

We are people in examples in these texts that try to help.

White Bears and Pink Elephants

Try right now ... not to think of ... – Daniel M Wegner

Please think of them! They've had a lifetime of
discouragement. Throw away all coconut ice, clear
shelves of marshmallow mix, do it properly: think
white = bear, pink = elephant. Disregard Cadillacs,
white leather seats, spurn Pink Ladies, platinum wigs.
Think powder puff endings to clinical psychologists
and theoretical cages which incarcerate white bears
and pink elephants with all the pies in the sky, their
four 'n' twenty blackbirds ready to surprise Week 1
of Group Therapy. Think up puffs of pink 'n' white
party smoke, focus the mind, think elephant = pink,
bear = white, kiss 'em, hug 'em, love bomb the hell
out of 'em, truly, madly bring 'em into the room, roar
'n' trumpet these bountiful beautiful beasts into being!

Notes

The epigraphs come from Emily Dickinson, poem 341, in *The Complete Poems*, ed. by Thomas H Johnson (London: Faber and Faber, 1975), p.162 and Edgar Allan Poe, 'The Imp of the Perverse', in *The Complete Tales and Poems of Edgar Allan Poe* (London: Penguin, 1982), pp.280–284: p.282.

'Body Found in Garden After Confession' is titled after a headline that appeared on the BBC News website in January 2018.

'The day my brain broke' is titled after an online article for BBC *Science Focus* magazine by James Lloyd published on 19 September 2017: https://www.sciencefocus.com/the-human-body/i-still-remember-the-day-my-brain-broke/

'Pure O' is titled after a term used to reference a form of OCD which seems to revolve around obsessions without observable compulsions. However, as James Lloyd writes in the article cited above, 'this internalised form of OCD is often called "Pure-O" (purely obsessional OCD), but this is something of a misnomer, as compulsions are still very much involved – they're just going on beneath the surface.' Associated compulsions include 'mental checking, mental chanting, repeating phrases or numbers in your head, scanning yourself or your environment, arguing with yourself, trying to solve the issue, avoidance of the thoughts, and ruminating,' writes Lauren Callaghan on p.164 of her book with Adam Shaw, *OCD, Anxiety, Panic Attacks and Related Depression: The Definitive Survival and Recovery Approach* (Newark: Trigger Press Ltd, 2016). In my own journey I've found Pure O a useful term for at least understanding more about these internal compulsions, an important step in realising I had OCD in the first place. See also, https://www.ocduk.org/ocd/pure-o/

'Contemporary Policemen in Their Homes' references, in the second stanza, Daniel M Wegner, *White Bears and Other Unwanted Thoughts: Suppression, Obsession, and the Psychology of Mental Control* (New York: The Guilford Press, 1994). See also, note to 'White Bears and Pink Elephants'.

'Safety-seeking Behaviours' is titled after a term described in David Veale and Rob Willson, *Overcoming Obsessive Compulsive Disorder: A self-help guide using Cognitive Behavioural Techniques* (London: Constable & Robinson Ltd, 2005), pp.15–16.

'Fear Brain' names its persona after a character who appears in a Psychology Tools handout entitled 'Intrusive thoughts – Why do they persist? A tale of two brains metaphor', devised by Kieran Fleck (2012).

'The Other Side of the Quarter Panel Mirror' is, in part, inspired by a line from Elizabeth Bishop's poem 'The Moose': '"Curious creatures" [...] "Look at that, would you."' Elizabeth Bishop, 'The Moose', in *Complete Poems* (London: Chatto and Windus, 1991), pp.169–173: p.173.

'Theory A, Theory B' is titled after, and inspired by, a technique used in cognitive behavioural therapy (CBT) for the treatment of OCD as exemplified in Dr Fiona Challacombe, Dr Victoria Bream Oldfield and Professor Paul Salkovskis, *Break Free From OCD: Overcoming Obsessive Compulsive Disorder with CBT* (Vermilion, 2011), pp.135–153.

Column one of 'The Thoughts' is, in part, a creative rearrangement of a handout entitled 'Normal intrusive thoughts', derived from research by C Purdon and DA Clark, 'Obsessive intrusive thoughts in nonclinical subjects. Part 1. Content and relation with depressive, anxious and obsessional symptoms,' *Behaviour Research and Therapy*, Nov 31(8), 1993, pp.713–720.

Columns two and three of 'The Thoughts' are, in part, a creative rearrangement of elements of the Obsessive-Compulsive Inventory, a self-report instrument outlined by E.B. Foa, M.J. Kozak et al., 'The Validation of a New Obsessive-Compulsive Disorder Scale: The Obsessive-Compulsive Inventory', *Psychological Assessment*, 10(3), 1998: pp.206–214.

'Exposure', 'Response' and 'Prevention' refer to a type of CBT known as Exposure and Response Prevention (ERP) used in the treatment of OCD. For more details see https://iocdf.org/about-ocd/ocd-treatment/erp/. A definition that has helped me is from Jon Hershfield and Shala Nicely who say that ERP 'works by having you gradually put yourself in the presence of the thoughts, feelings, or experiences that cause you discomfort (exposure) while resisting attempts to use physical or mental compulsions to neutralize or avoid the discomfort (response prevention)' – see *Everyday Mindfulness for OCD: Tips, Tricks & Skills for Living Joyfully* (Oakland, CA: New Harbinger Publications, 2017), p.4.

'Subjective Units of Distress' (also known as 'Standard Units of Distress' and, commonly, 'SUDs') is a distress scale used within CBT with ERP whereby the person with OCD symptoms rates their distress in a given exposure task. In '16/17' creative use is made of a scale 'ranging from 0 (no distress at all) to 100 (the most distress an obsession can cause you)' – see Christine Purdon and David A. Clark in *Overcoming Obsessive Thoughts: How to Gain Control of Your OCD* (Oakland, CA: New Harbinger Publications, 2005), p.120.

'17/17' derives its format from what is known as the 'hot cross bun' analogy of the CBT model, first developed by Christine Paredsky. Professor Shirley Reynolds deftly illustrates this in a video at https://www.futurelearn.com/courses/anxiety-depression-and-cbt/0/steps/14736

'Examples' creatively rearranges, in part, obsessions and compulsions discussed in the following: David Adam, *The Man Who Couldn't Stop: OCD, and the True Story of a Life Lost in Thought* (London: Picador, 2014), p.3; Shaw and Callaghan, p.48; and Veale and Willson p.123.

'White Bears and Pink Elephants' has its origins in research on thought suppression and mental control developed by Wegner in *White Bears and Other Unwanted Thoughts* (see note to 'Contemporary Policemen in Their Homes'). Following this groundbreaking research, many have been encouraged to test out its core theory in advice like Wegner's: 'Try right now, for instance, not to think of a white bear. Really. Put down the book and look away and stop thinking of a white bear' (Wegner p.1). However, the very attempt to *not think* of something makes you think of it, more than you would if you *weren't* trying to suppress the thought. It's not clear where and when white bears were supplemented by pink elephants, but the latter are perhaps more commonplace in the reading I have done and certainly part of my own treatment experience.

Further Reading

International OCD Federation (IOCDF), https://iocdf.org/

NHS, https://www.nhs.uk/mental-health/conditions/obsessive-compulsive-disorder-ocd/overview/

OCD Action, https://ocdaction.org.uk/

OCD UK, https://www.ocduk.org/

Acknowledgements

Thank you to the following publications where some of these poems – or versions of them – first appeared: *Brittle Star, Envoi, Fenland Poetry Journal, Finished Creatures, Live Canon 2018 Anthology, Orbis, Poetry Wales, The Rialto, Shearsman, Tears in the Fence, Truths: A Telltale Press Anthology, Under the Radar* and *The White Review*.

'Body Found in Garden After Confession' and 'Newly in love, distracted neuroscientists ♥' were winning poems in the Poetry Society Members' Poems Competitions (2021, 2018) and first published in *Poetry News*.

Thank you to everyone at The Poetry Business and especially to Suzannah Evans and Gboyega Odubanjo for making the book (and me) work harder – and better. I am deeply grateful.

Thank you to Stephen Bone, Jane Commane, Abigail Parry and Catherine Smith: I have learned from all of you. Thank you to Heidi Beck, Kate Hendry, Tess Jolly and Mary Wight for truthful – crucial – conversations in the latter stages of this book: I have learned from you too.

Thank you to Robin Houghton and Peter Kenny for coaxing me out of my cupboard, where I was alone eating crisps, into the daylight of Telltale Press.

Thank you to the NHS and especially to the OCD clinic in Brighton and Hove for remarkable care and kindness.

Thank you to Elizabeth J. Bell, Maura Dooley, Jo Emerson, Sally McManus and Katrina Naomi for long friendship and wisdom.

Thank you to Rachel Brown, Angela Buxton and Natasha Moscovici, who each rescued me when I needed them to.

Thank you to Zachary for important facts about Jupiter and for inventing – and performing exquisitely – the *Is it poetry?* family joke.

Thank you to Charlotte Gann: in our talk there are many taverns.

Thank you to Di Shields: you know why.

Thank you – and all my love – to Louise Tondeur: still the one.